A Romantic Meal for Two

A Romantic Meal for Two

by Sam Stafford

Photography by Nicolas Laborie

Illustrations by Bill Ledger

Published by Max Budgett

First published in Great Britain in 2005
by Tmax Productions Ltd
www.tmaxbooks.co.uk

Printed and bound in Great Britain by Butler & Tanner Ltd

Author - Sam Stafford
Photographer - Nicolas Laborie
Illustrator - Bill Ledger
Publisher - Max Budgett

Acknowledgments
Many thanks to Anne, Greg, Andrew, Emil, Matt, Lynn, Poppy, Nille, Carole, Tom, Michael, Philippa, Lizzie and Jess

ISBN 0-9549402-0-2

Contents

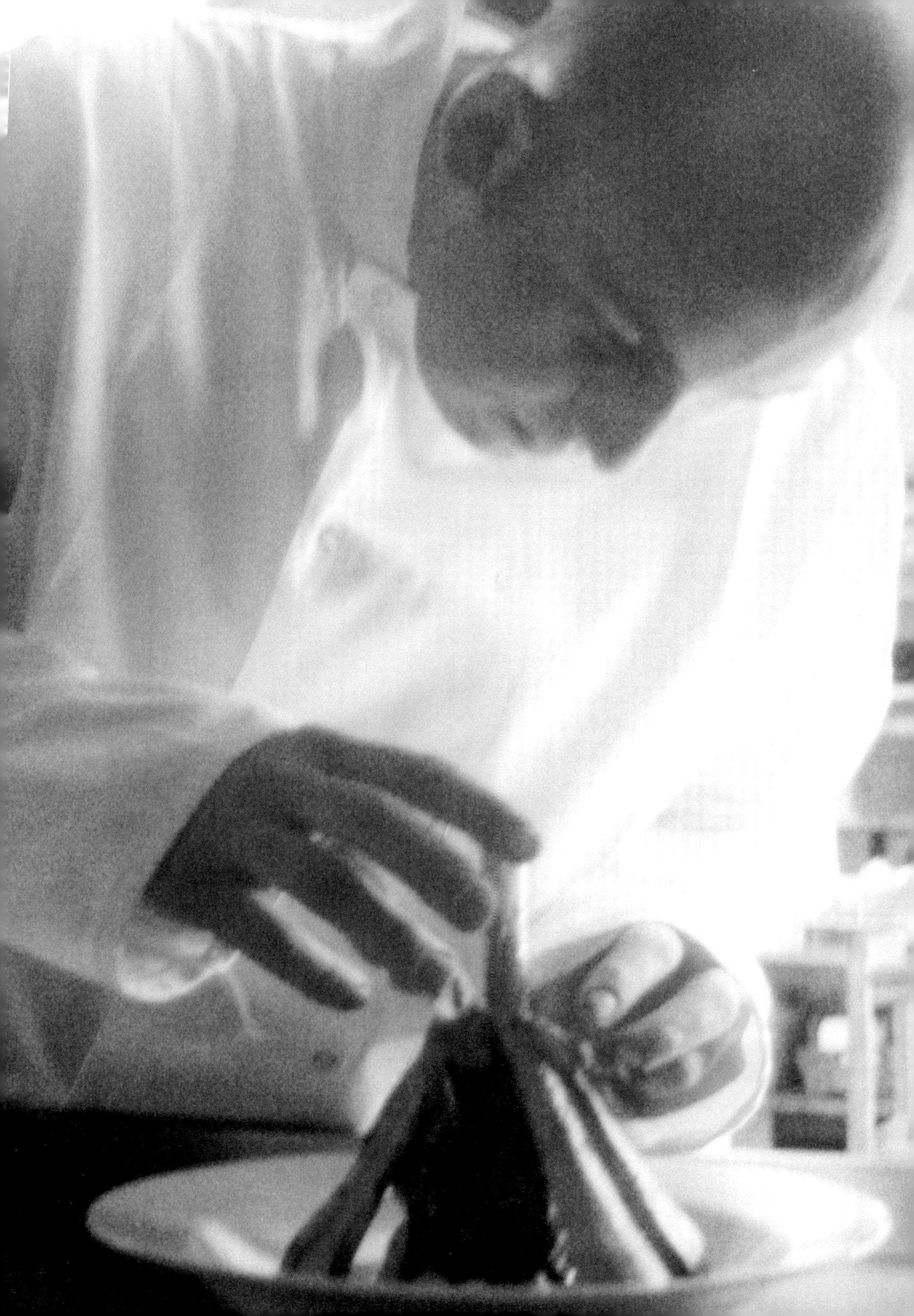

Introduction

Hello. So you have bought this DVD cookbook and now want to cook a tasty meal for your loved one. Cheesy as it might sound, cooking a meal for someone is a great way to show you care about them. Let me give you an example; my best mate Matt had just started dating his girlfriend before Valentine's Day last year. He rang me up and told me that he wanted to cook her a romantic meal for Valentine's Day. One problem, he can't cook to save his life. I talked him through a simple but impressive looking meal step-by-step. The result was fabulous, she loved it and they are still together today. Result.

I want you to understand that what you will learn is not only these dishes, but also techniques that you will be able to use with other dishes. Once you know how to cook the Lamb Shank, for example, you can apply the same principles to another meat that is suited to braising, such as a brisket of beef.

Attention and instinct are two other skills that are important in cooking. Times are just guidelines. If it says 2-3 hours it is only to give you an idea. At the restaurant I don't work to times, I simply check whatever I am cooking every few minutes. Feel, touch, take a bite, taste it and then you will learn when something is almost ready and when it is there. What many cookbooks don't take into account is that not every stove and oven is exactly the same, some cook hotter and faster than others. This will affect your cooking times. Use your instincts; if it looks and feels ready it is reasonably safe to say that it is. Trust yourself. Have confidence.

Last but not least, put some love and care into your cooking. A happy loving kitchen will produce good food. Just go for it. We all make mistakes and might not produce perfection, but as long as it looks good and tastes even better, you have the day!

STARTERS

Smoked duck with horseradish potato salad, satsumas and honey dressing

Ingredients

1	Packet of Smoked Duck
2	Medium White Potatoes
2	Tablespoons of Mayonnaise
1	Teaspoon of Horseradish
1	Tablespoon of Chopped Parsley
1	Satsuma
30g	Salad Leaves

Vinaigrette

3	Tablespoons of Olive Oil
1	Tablespoon of White Wine Vinegar
1	Teaspoon Honey Thyme
	Salt and Pepper

Smoked duck is my favourite of the smoked and cured meats. Smoking duck gives it a great flavour that really works. There is now top quality smoked duck available from supermarkets and markets. I smoke my own at the restaurant but it is quite hard work and very smoky. Duck and orange is a real 70's combination, some say not a good one. I think that here it works, as the sweet and sour of the satsuma cuts the smoke of the duck. We will soon find out if you agree. This dish is more about presentation than hard work in the kitchen.

1. Prepare the potatoes

Peel the potatoes and cut them into small cubes. Place them in a saucepan of water with a good pinch of salt. Put the saucepan on the stove and bring the water to the boil. Be careful, once the potatoes are boiling they will not take long to cook, only around 10 minutes. Check them regularly. Take a cube out and try. They must retain cooked but firm texture, don't let them cook to mush. Once the potatoes are ready, run them under cold water to stop them cooking. Then drain them, shake off the excess water and put them in a bowl.

2. The potato salad

Now add the mayonnaise and horseradish cream and mix well. Season. Chop the parsley as finely as you can and add to the potato salad.

3. Make the vinaigrette

Put salt, pepper, vinegar and thyme leaves in a jar and add a teaspoon of honey. Give it a good shake. Add the oil and repeat. Adjust seasoning to your taste. You might like more honey?

4. And the satsuma

Peel the satsuma and separate the segments.

5. Presenting the dish

Place a plastic ring (*see Hints and Tips section*) in the centre of the plate, pack the potato salad into it firmly and remove the ring. Push three segments of satsuma into the salad (*see photo*). Now open the duck and carefully arrange a few slices on top of the potatoes. Place a few leaves of salad on top of the duck (use salad straight from the packet). Give the vinaigrette a good shake and spoon it around the dish. Serve.

Leaf salad with poached pear, Roquefort, baby new potatoes and pear vinaigrette

Ingredients

1	Bag of Mixed Salad Leaves
1	Pear
400ml	Water
100g	Sugar
1	Star Anise
4	Cloves
250g	Roquefort
8	Baby New Potatoes

Vinaigrette

1	Tablespoon of White Wine Vinegar
3	Tablespoons of Olive Oil
2	Tablespoons of Pear Juice
	Salt and Pepper

This salad is a classic. It is sophisticated and luscious. Roquefort is a fabulous French ewe's milk cheese that is aged in caves. It is a strong blue cheese that is salty and creamy. Pear is the perfect accompaniment and the new potatoes bring a different texture to the salad. This salad is quite literally to die for.

If you don't like blue cheese, then goat's cheese is a good replacement.

Tuna Tartar, avocado, baby plum tomatoes and chive mayonnaise

Ingredients

120g	Tuna
2	Spring Onions
½	Avocado
6-8	Baby Plum Tomatoes
	Lemon Juice
1	Tablespoon of Mayonnaise
	Chopped Chives

Vinaigrette

3	Tablespoons of Olive Oil
1	Tablespoon White Wine Vinegar
	Pinch of Sugar
	Salt and Pepper

If you are feeling 'in the money' you could add a bit of caviar to the top for even more luxury.

I love raw fish. Sushi and sashimi are particular favourites and tuna is at the top of my list. It has a great texture that has a bit of a bite but is ultimately smooth. I know that raw fish is not to everyone's taste and that is fine; however, if you are just a little doubtful, give it a go! If the fact that it is raw really turns your stomach, then you can simply add some lemon juice and the acid in the lemon will cook the fish. Traditionally, tartar refers to a raw beef preparation, which incidentally is also delicious. Many of the elements that make that dish delicious are included in this one; hence, I have called it tartar.

1. Prepare the fish

Order or buy really fresh tuna. **DO NOT BUY IT** if it does not smell clean and fresh or has a rainbow effect on the flesh. Very dark tuna means that it has a lot of blood in the flesh from when the fish was killed, again avoid it. You want a nice light red colour. Talk to the fishmonger or the person serving at the counter in the supermarket and ask about the fish.

Take your tuna and dice the flesh into small cubes. It does not matter if your cubes are not perfect as long as they are small. Place the tuna in a bowl.

2. Prepare the avocado and spring onions

Repeat the same process with the avocado. Cut it in half, remove the stone and the skin, and dice. Place in the same bowl as the tuna and mix. Thinly slice the spring onions and add them to the mixture.

3. Lemon juice

At this stage you can add the lemon juice. It is entirely up to you. I would add just a tiny squeeze for my own taste. Season with salt and pepper and taste.

4. Arrange the tomatoes

Slice the baby plum tomatoes lengthwise and carefully arrange them in a circle on the plate. This is just how I would present it in the restaurant. If you want to cut them differently and do your own thing, go ahead.

5. Vinaigrette

Vinaigrette is so simple. Place the salt, pepper and sugar in a screw top jar with the vinegar and give it a good shake (with the lid on). Then add the olive oil and shake it again. Give it a taste. Done!

6. Chive mayonnaise

With scissors, snip the chives and mix 2/3 with the mayonnaise. Save the remainder for garnish.

7. Presenting the dish

Place a plastic ring (*see Hints and Tips section*) in the centre of the tomatoes and fill almost to the top with the tuna mix. Fill the remaining bit with the chive mayonnaise and smooth off. Remove the ring carefully. Drizzle some vinaigrette around the plate and sprinkle some chives.

MAIN COURSES

Braised lamb shank with cumin scented mash, sweet roasted parsnip and braising sauce

Ingredients

2	Lamb Shanks
1	Onion
1	Carrot
½	Leek
2	Stalks of Celery
1-2	Cloves of Garlic
1	Bay Leaf
4	Sprigs of Thyme
2	Large Parsnips
1	Tablespoon Tomato Puree
800g	Mashing Potatoes
90g	Butter
	Cumin
	Salt and Pepper

Lamb is a great meat that I enjoy cooking in a variety of ways. Braising is the method that is best suited to its shank. Braising is a great method of cooking that lends itself to the winter and warm hearty dishes. Once you can braise a shank you will be able to use the same method with other cuts of meat. Braising is deeply satisfying and produces great aromas and flavour which will leave you a convert. An added bonus is that you are able to braise your meat in advance; in fact, if the meat is left to cool and remain in its braising liquor for a couple of days in the fridge, it actually improves.

1. Prepare the vegetables

Peel all the vegetables except for the parsnips. Cut them up roughly and add them to a deep saucepan with a splash of vegetable oil and fry gently for at least 10 minutes until they are nicely coloured.

2. Fry the lamb shanks

Season your lamb shanks and fry them in a frying pan until golden all round.

3. Cook the lamb shanks

Add the tomato puree to the vegetables, mix and fry for a further few minutes. Be careful, tomato puree burns easily. Now add the shanks and enough water to cover them. You may either leave this pot on the stove to cook, or cover with tin foil and put it in the oven at 160°C for 2½ hours, checking after 2 hours. If you cook it on the stove, be sure to reduce the heat and always top up the liquid if needed. This will take around the same amount of time.

4. Roast the parsnips

Peel and cut the parsnips into quarters. Place them on a baking tray and drizzle with oil, season and dust with a pinch of ground cumin. Place in the oven at 180°C - 200°C and roast until nice and golden.

5. Make the mash

Peel the potatoes and place in a saucepan of boiling water with a pinch of salt. Simmer until the potatoes are tender and soft, then drain and mash with butter. Add butter to taste. Season well and add a teaspoon of cumin. Stir it through. Taste it. Add more if you desire.

6. The shanks are ready

You will know when the lamb shanks are cooked - they will be very tender and almost falling off the bone. Remove them from the liquid and strain the vegetables. Now cook the liquid until it has reduced by 2/3. This is your sauce. If the shanks are being prepared in advance, allow the sauce to cool. Now place the shanks in a container and cover with the cooled sauce. Cover with cling film and store in the fridge. The sauce will set; this is natural.

7. Presenting the dish

Place a mound of mash in the centre of a plate, then the shank on top and then the parsnips. Cover with sauce and garnish with chopped parsley.

Spaghetti with Palourdes Clams and tomato sauce

Ingredients

1kg	Clams (Palourdes)
180g	Spaghetti
1	Red Chilli
1	Clove of Garlic
1	Small Onion
3	Sprigs of Thyme
1	Bay Leaf
6-8	Ripe Tomatoes
½	Bunch of Parsley
	Olive oil
	Salt and Pepper

Wow, I love this dish. Love it, love it, love it. Clams are delicious. Their flavour is clean and sea like. My girlfriend and I have eaten a kilo and a half just as a midnight snack and it was the best. Please make the effort to find them. Supermarkets will order items for you; if you have a local fishmonger go to them or go to a market. Buy fresh smelling, firmly closed clams and enjoy one of the finest shellfish around.

1. Throw out the dead clams

Give the clams a good rinse and check for any broken ones. If the shells are broken, throw them away. If you find any that are open, give them a tap on a surface - if they close, all is well, but if they don't they are dead and should be thrown away. Clams must be alive when they are cooked. If you eat dead ones there is a possibility that they could make you ill and you don't want that on your romantic evening.

2. Chop chop chop

Finely dice the onion and garlic. Slice the chilli. Most of the heat of a chilli is in its seeds and pith, so if you don't want the dish to be too hot you can remove these. Again, only use as much as you want, there are no rules.

3. Cook your pasta

Place a large saucepan of water on the stove and bring to the boil. Once the water is boiling, add a good pinch of salt. Pasta cooking times vary, so please refer to the cooking guidelines on the packet of pasta. The pasta needs to be cooked al dente, but what does that mean? You probably cook it al dente anyway, since overcooked or undercooked pasta is really not very nice. The pasta is ready when you can bite into it and it has a firm but cooked through texture. Trying it regularly while it is cooking is the key to getting it right.

4. Pasta in advance

If you are preparing the pasta in advance, run it under cold water when it is ready, to stop it cooking. Drain and coat lightly in olive oil. Cover and put this in the fridge. You can prepare the pasta up to a day in advance. To re-heat, simply pour boiling water straight from the kettle over it and leave for a minute. Drain.

5. Time to fry

Pour a good slug of olive oil, not loads, but enough to coat the bottom of the frying pan. On a low to medium heat, warm the oil, then add the onions, garlic and chilli, as well as the thyme and bay leaf. Fry gently for five or so minutes, until they go a nice golden brown colour.

6. Cook the clams and serve

Dice the tomatoes and add to the pan. Cook for just a few minutes, no more than five. Add the clams. Give the pan a good stir through and leave to cook. The clams are ready when they have all opened up, but be aware that the odd one may have been dead from the start, therefore has not opened and should be thrown away.

Season your dish, but remember that the clams are salty, so not too much salt. Finally add the chopped parsley and serve.

Large roasted onion stuffed with roasted winter vegetables, accompanied by spiced couscous and cucumber salsa

Ingredients

2 Large Onions
1 Turnip
2 Carrots
2 Parsnips
1 Butternut Squash
1 Red Onion
2 Garlic Cloves
4 Sprigs of Thyme
Vegetable Oil

Salsa

½ Cucumber
8 Cherry Tomatoes
2 Spring Onions
1 Tablespoon of Chopped Parsley
Olive Oil

Couscous

120g Couscous
250ml Boiling Water
1 Teaspoon Ras-El Hanout
1 Tablespoon Olive Oil
1 Tablespoon Chopped Chives

This is a great looking and interesting vegetarian dish. It is an adaptation of a dish I once saw that had a stuffing of veal sweetbreads. Here the offal is replaced with roasted vegetables and paired with a really fresh salsa and couscous. Couscous has a bad reputation for being tasteless. I think when you try it with some spices and herbs, you'll find it to be a great accompaniment to all sorts of dishes. Give it a go!

Note: All elements of this dish can be prepared in advance

1. Prepare the onions

Bring a saucepan of water to the boil. Remove the roots from the onions, but do not peel them. Prick the ends with a knife. Put the onions in the water and simmer for 10-15 minutes.

2. Roast the onions

Remove the onions from the water and place them on an oven tray. Roast them in the oven for 45-60 minutes at 200°C until they feel soft inside. Remove and allow to cool.

3. Roast the vegetables

Peel and chop the vegetables for roasting. Place a roasting tray in the oven or on the stove with a splash of vegetable oil. Add the vegetables one by one starting with the carrots. Once all the vegetables are in the tray, add the thyme and place in the oven at the same time as the onions (they will take the same time to cook) and roast for 30 minutes. Check. Now cook for a further 15-30 minutes. Once cooked, allow to cool and season.

4. Make the salsa

Remove the cucumber seeds, carefully dice the cucumber and place in a bowl. Dice the tomatoes, chop the spring onions and place them in the same bowl. Finally chop the parsley and add. Season with salt and pepper, and add the olive oil. Mix well and taste. If you wish, add a squeeze of lemon juice or a tablespoon of white wine vinegar to give the salsa some acidity. This is up to you, but personally I prefer to keep the flavour very fresh.

5. Make the couscous

Place all the couscous ingredients in a bowl, apart from the water and chives. Add a pinch of salt and a twist of pepper. Now add the boiling water straight from the kettle and stir. Cover with cling film and leave in a warm place for 20 minutes. Allow to cool completely. Once cold, break up the grains with your fingers. Add the chives and check for seasoning.

6. Stuff the onions

Once the onions and roast vegetables have cooked, leave them to cool. Once cooled, take some scissors and cut the top off the onion. Do not throw this away. Now carefully remove the inside of the onions and place the onion skins on a square of tin foil. Now stuff the onions with roast vegetables and when full place the lid back on. Wrap the onions in tin foil and put them back in the oven at 220°C for 15-20 minutes until hot.

7. Presenting the dish

The couscous can be served either hot or cold. If you like it hot, then just heat through in the microwave for a minute or two (personally I like it cold). Place the couscous in the centre of the plate and put the onion on top. Spoon the salsa around the plate and garnish with flat leaf parsley.

DESSERTS

Banoffee pie with Baileys cream

Ingredients

130g	Digestive Biscuits
60g	Butter
1	Tin of Condensed Milk
3-4	Bananas
350ml	Double Cream
1	Shot of Baileys

What can you say about Banoffee Pie that hasn't already been said? All that toffee, bananas and cream. Pure heaven. I have put this dish on several menus and people love it, it is one of the most popular desserts I know. The true proof of its greatness as a pudding is that the waitresses always beg for a slice after work. Without fail!

You can either make a large cake and cut individual slices or for something a little special why not make individual portions (see picture)

Passion fruit jelly with homemade yoghurt ice cream

Jelly Ingredients

3-4 Passion Fruits
60g Caster Sugar
200ml Water
3-5 Leaves of Leaf Gelatine (see method)
Lemon Juice

Ice Cream Ingredients

250g Set Yoghurt
250g Caster Sugar
250g Double Cream

Yoghurt ice cream is so simple to make and you can do any variations you want. All you need is equal quantities of the listed ingredients and multiply them as you require.

Passion fruit is my favourite fruit. It has everything, it is sweet and sour with great flavour and texture. In short, it rocks. Jellies are simple to make and fun. Who didn't love jelly and ice cream as a kid? I loved it and still do! Your imagination is your only limit when it comes to making jellies. They don't have to be sweet, it is up to you. Just remember, 4-5 sheets of gelatine to 500ml of liquid. You can't go wrong. When presenting your jellies you can use anything to hand: wine glasses, plastic water cups, cocktail glasses and shot glasses, as I have done.

1. Selecting your passion fruits

Look for wrinkled and dimpled passion fruits; this means they are ripe. Cut them in half and squeeze the fruit's contents into a saucepan. A teaspoon will help to get the last bits. Leave all the pips in for now.

2. Add sugar and water

Once all the fruit is safely in the pan, weigh the sugar and add. Finally, add water.

3. Cook the jelly mix

Place the pan on a stove and bring to the boil. When the water is boiling, turn the heat down to a gentle simmer. Let it simmer for 2 minutes or until all the sugar has dissolved. Remove from the stove and leave to one side whilst the flavours develop.

4. Add gelatine

Now, soak the leaf gelatine in cold water until it goes soft. Do not leave it for too long or the gelatine will start to disintegrate. Once it has softened, lift it out with your hands and squeeze out any excess water. Add the gelatine to the jelly liquid and whisk it to make sure it is well incorporated.

5. How many seeds would you like?

This bit is entirely up to you. You can now strain the mix through a sieve and remove the seeds. This allows you to add back as many as you would like. This depends entirely on your taste. Personally I find that too many seeds produce a jelly with too much 'crunch', so I add just a few seeds to the mixture as this makes it look good and gives added texture without ruining the smoothness of the jelly.

6. The jelly mould

You may now pour the jelly mixture into a mould. This can be anything you desire. For this demonstration I have used a shot glass. Put the mould into the fridge and leave it to set for a minimum of two hours (depending on the size of your mould).

7. Serve

Serve the jelly with cream, crème fraiche or ice cream.

8. Yoghurt ice cream

Blend or whisk all the ingredients and place in the freezer. If you wish, add the same weight of fruit as the other ingredients (250g). You may also want to try adding Maltesers or pieces of chocolate.

Chocolate fudge cake

Ingredients

120g	Bitter Chocolate (70% Cocoa Solids)
100g	Butter
100g	Sugar
3	Tablespoons of Self Raising Flour
3	Eggs, Separated

This chocolate cake is my mother's recipe, I am proud to say. When she makes it, the cake never survives beyond tea. Everyone has to have a second slice and, in my case, a third. It is one of the best chocolate cakes I have ever eaten. When I recently put this cake on the menu at the restaurant with bramley apple in it, I was only just able to keep up with production. The beauty of this cake is that you don't need a cake tin to cook it in, all you need is a frying pan and some baking paper. Quite an unusual way of baking a cake, but the result is fabulous.

1. Melt the chocolate

Place a saucepan that is half full of water on the stove and bring to a simmer. This will produce steam that we will use for melting the chocolate. Place a heatproof bowl containing the chocolate and the butter on top of the saucepan. Allow the mixture to melt.

2. Separate the eggs

Separate the eggs into yolks and whites by moving the yolk between the two shells, letting the white drop into a bowl.

3. Prepare the frying pan

Lightly butter a medium frying pan and line with a circle of greaseproof paper. This is what we are going to cook the cake in.

4. Add yolks, sugar and flour

Once the chocolate and butter have melted, add the yolks one by one whilst stirring continuously. Then add the sugar a little bit at a time and repeat with the flour.

5. Whip the egg whites

Whip the egg whites until stiff and fold bit by bit into the chocolate mixture. Use a metal spoon, like a serving spoon, to fold in the mixture. This will ensure that you do not knock the air out of the whites. Add to the frying pan.

6. Cook the cake

Cook the cake for 20-25 minutes at 140°C. The cake should be nice and springy in the middle.

7. Serve

Allow the cake to cool and serve with ice-cream, cream, chocolate sauce or just how it is.

Seasoning

Chefs in books and on TV all say: Season with salt and pepper to taste. What do they mean? Salt and pepper bring flavour out of food. Salt is highly corrosive; just think of the seaside and you will realise that metal that is near the sea is always corroded by salt. This property of salt draws out flavour in ingredients. However, you do not actually want to taste the salt - if you do, then the dish is over salted. Pepper is spicy and brings a slight heat to food. Combined with salt it can change bland food into something very tasty. It is all about balance.

You also need to consider that all our tastes are different. As a professional you need to learn to find a universal level and be quite brave about it. My father likes a lot of salt in his food, hence my mother has learnt to season to his palate and as a result her mashed potatoes, for example, are gorgeous, but too salty for my taste.

Seasoning is where home cooks (and often restaurant chefs) go wrong. You have followed a recipe and it has all worked out but tastes bland - why? Seasoning. I suggest you make some mashed potatoes with only a little salt in the cooking water, then season them little by little adding salt and pepper. Taste it, then add a little more until the flavour of the potatoes comes alive in your mouth. Now you are there.

Seasoning, to confuse things even more, doesn't just mean salt and pepper. Other things bring out flavour as well. Worcester sauce with tomatoes or cheese, for example. The reason I am telling you this is so that you can experiment with things that work for you. Your imagination is your only limit.

A final word: Be brave with your seasoning and take it stage by stage and it will happen.

Hints and Tips

1. Buy the very best ingredients that you can afford
2. Use sharp knives
3. Take your time and don't rush
4. Prepare as much as you can in advance:

You will want to spend as much time with your loved one as possible during your romantic meal, so be sure to prepare as much as you can in advance.

5. Folding egg white:

Always use a metal spoon when folding egg white into a mixture, not a wooden spoon (*see DVD for technique*). The metal spoon has a sharper edge that will cut through the egg white. This will ensure that you do not knock the air out of the white, that you so painstakingly whisked to get in there in the first place.

6. Use a plastic ring for presentation:

Why not use a piece of plastic drainage pipe as your presentation ring? You can use anything to help you mould your food into eye catching shapes. I frequently use a cylinder shaped piece of plastic drainage pipe to shape the tuna tartar and duck dishes, for example.

Centigrade	Gas Mark	Description
105	1/4	Very cool
120	1/2	Very cool
130	1	Cool
150	2	Cool
165	3	Very moderate
180	4	Moderate
190	5	Moderate
200	6	Moderately hot
220	7	Hot
230	8	Hot
245	9	Very hot

Menu

Starters

p11 *Smoked duck with horseradish potato salad, satsumas and honey dressing*

p14 *Leaf salad with poached pear, Roquefort, baby new potatoes and pear vinaigrette*

p19 *Tuna tartar, avocado, baby plum tomatoes and chive mayonnaise*

Main Courses

p25 *Braised lamb shank with cumin scented mash, sweet roasted parsnip and braising sauce*

p28 *Spaghetti with Palourdes clams and tomato sauce*

p33 *Large roasted onion stuffed with roasted winter vegetables, accompanied by spiced couscous and cucumber salsa*

Desserts

p39 *Banoffee pie*

p42 *Passion fruit jelly with homemade yoghurt ice cream*

p47 *Chocolate fudge cake*

Free DVD

This DVD contains step-by-step cooking guidelines to all dishes featured in this book.

Created by Tmax Productions Ltd
www.tmaxbooks.co.uk

DVD Replication by Databiz

Featuring chef Sam Stafford

To receive the latest information on future DVD Cookbooks visit www.tmaxbooks.co.uk

With thanks to Sam Smith and Julian Elkan